ELLIOTT CARTER

STRING TRIO

for violin, viola, and violoncello

HENDON MUSIC

BOOSEY & HAWKES

AN **IMAGEM** COMPANY

DISTRIBUTED BY

HAL•LEONARD®
CORPORATION

7777 W. BLUEMOUND RD. P.O. BOX 13819 MILWAUKEE, WI 53213

www.boosey.com
www.halleonard.com

Published by Hendon Music, Inc.
a Boosey & Hawkes company
229 West 28th Street, 11th Fl
New York, NY
10001

www.boosey.com

AN IMAGEM COMPANY

ISMN: 979-0-051-10713-1

First printed: July 2011
Second printing with revisions: December 2011

For Rolf, Richard and Fred

First performed on December 8, 2011 at the
Kaufmann Concert Hall – 92nd Street Y in New York City
by Rolf Schulte, violin; Richard O'Neill, viola; Fred Sherry, cello

Duration: 7 minutes

PROGRAM NOTE

In planning to compose this string trio I realized that the viola had a more somber sound than the more brilliant violin and cello. While held like the violin, it is somewhat larger which forces the fingers that stop the strings to reach further for high notes. Therefore, I felt that I would make the viola have its own voice and be the most prominent member of the ensemble. The work is dedicated to Rolf Schulte, Richard O'Neill and Fred Sherry. It was composed in May, 2011.

—Elliott Carter
October 27, 2011

ANMERKUNGEN DES KOMPONISTEN

Bei meiner Planung für die Komposition dieses Streichtrios bemerkte ich, dass die Viola einen trauervolleren Klang hat als die strahlend klingende Violine und das Cello. Sie wird genauso gespielt wie die Violine, ist aber etwas größer, was die Finger dazu zwingt, bei den hohen Noten weiter zu greifen. Deshalb beschloss ich, dass die Bratsche, die ihre eigene Stimme haben sollte, das bedeutendste Ensemblemitglied ist. Das Stück ist Rolf Schulte, Richard O'Neill und Fred Sherry gewidmet. Es wurde im Mai 2011 komponiert.

—Elliott Carter
27. Oktober 2011

NOTE DE PROGRAMME

Lors de la planification de la composition de ce trio à cordes, je me suis rendu compte que l'alto avait un son plus sombre que le violon et le violoncelle qui eux sont plus éclatants. Bien que tenu comme un violon, il est quelque peu plus grand ce qui force les doigts qui appuient les cordes à chercher plus loin pour atteindre les notes aiguës. De ce fait, je me suis amené à confier sa propre voix à l'alto et à en faire le membre le plus éminent de l'ensemble. L'oeuvre est dédiée à Rolf Schulte, Richard O'Neill et Fred Sherry. Elle a été composée en mai 2011.

—Elliott Carter
27 octobre 2011

for Rolf, Richard, and Fred

STRING TRIO

Elliott Carter
(2011)

979–0–051–10713–1

Revised: December 2011

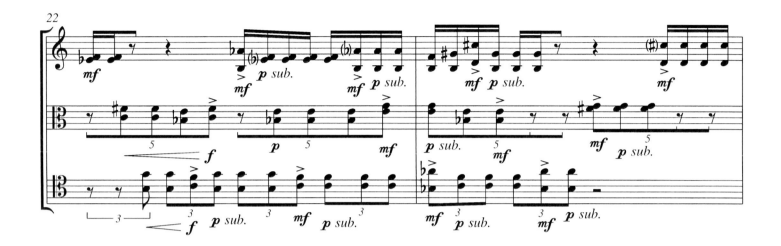

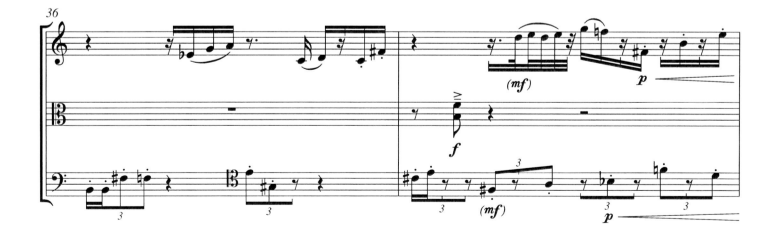

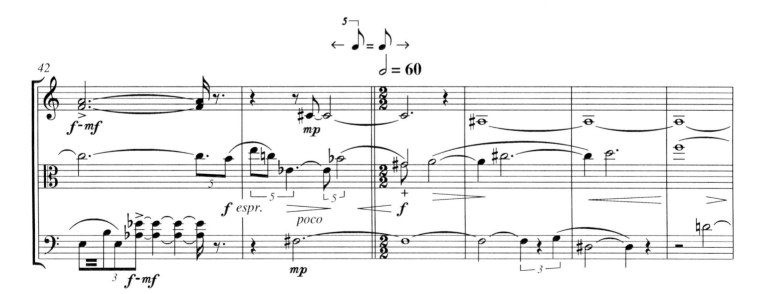

ELLIOTT CARTER

STRING TRIO

for violin, viola, and violoncello

HENDON MUSIC

BOOSEY & HAWKES

AN IMAGEM COMPANY

DISTRIBUTED BY

HAL•LEONARD®
CORPORATION
7777 W. BLUEMOUND RD. P.O. BOX 13819 MILWAUKEE, WI 53213

www.boosey.com
www.halleonard.com

for Rolf, Richard, and Fred

STRING TRIO

Violin

Elliott Carter
(2011)

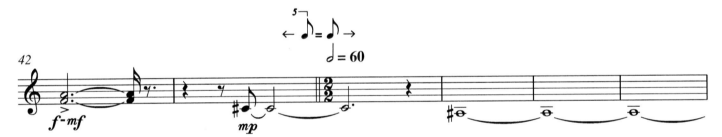

V.S.

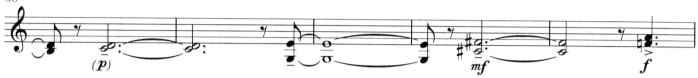

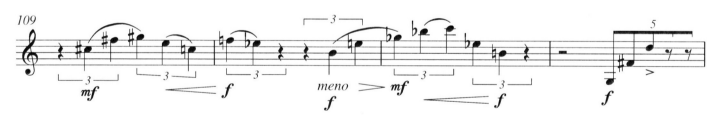

con intensità

119–122

VIOLONCELLO

ELLIOTT CARTER

STRING TRIO
for violin, viola, and violoncello

HENDON MUSIC
BOOSEY & HAWKES
AN IMAGEM COMPANY

DISTRIBUTED BY
HAL•LEONARD®
CORPORATION
7777 W. BLUEMOUND RD. P.O. BOX 13819 MILWAUKEE, WI 53213

www.boosey.com
www.halleonard.com

for Rolf, Richard, and Fred

STRING TRIO

Violoncello

Elliott Carter
(2011)

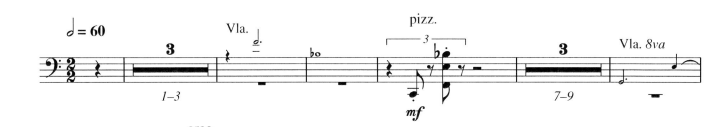

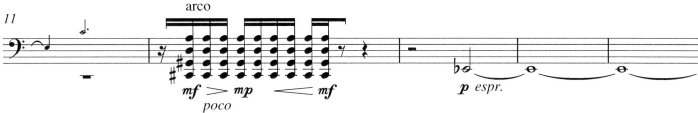

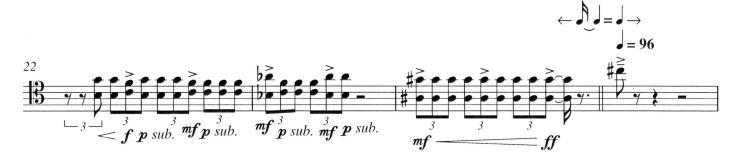

2

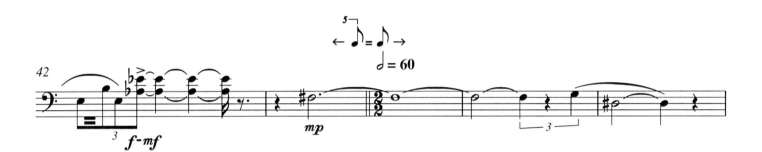

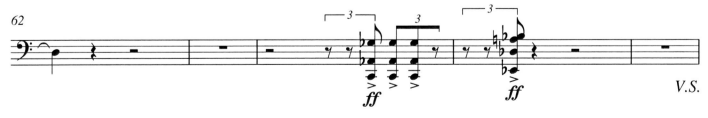

V.S.

119–122

for Rolf, Richard, and Fred

STRING TRIO

Viola

Elliott Carter
(2011)

Revised: December 2011

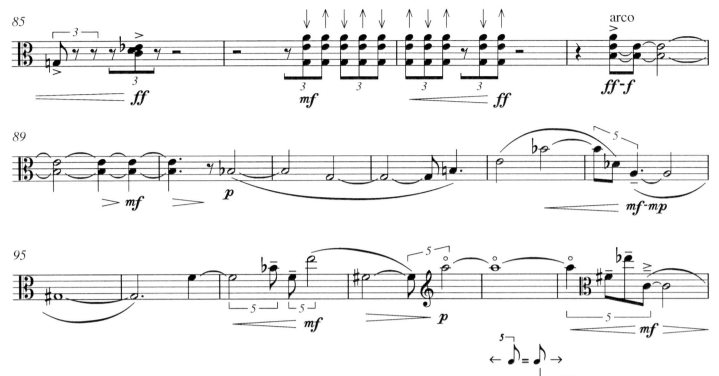

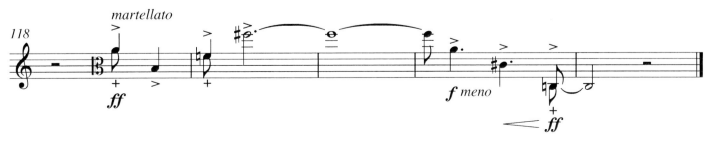

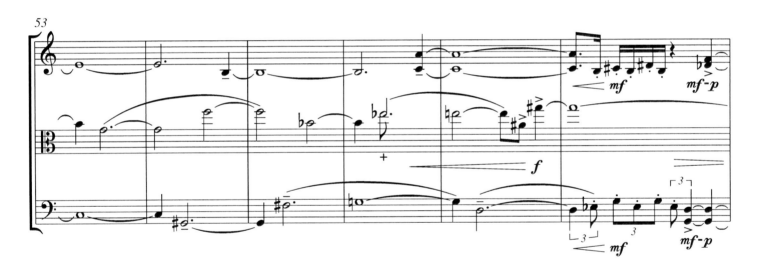
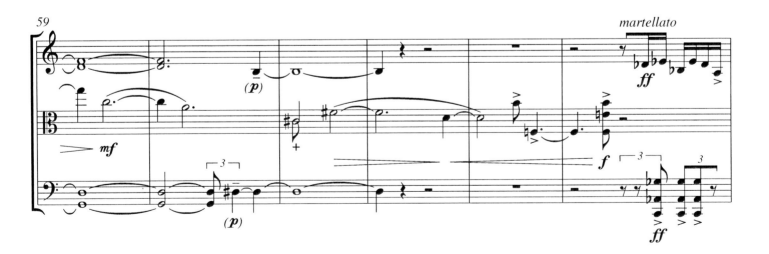

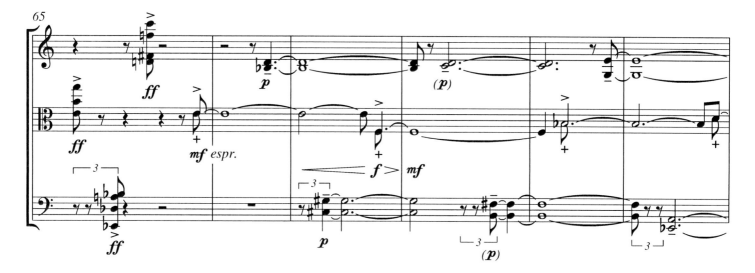

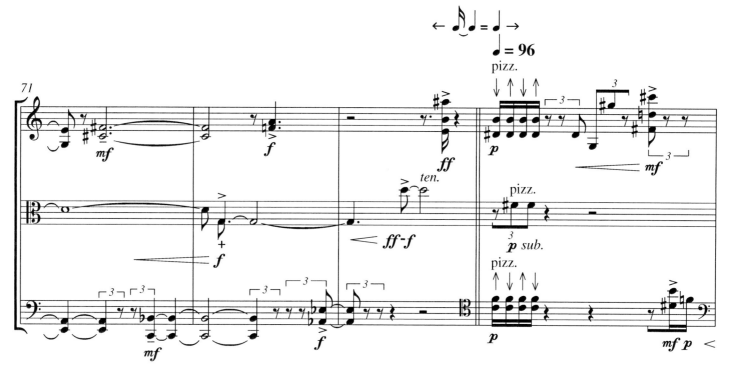

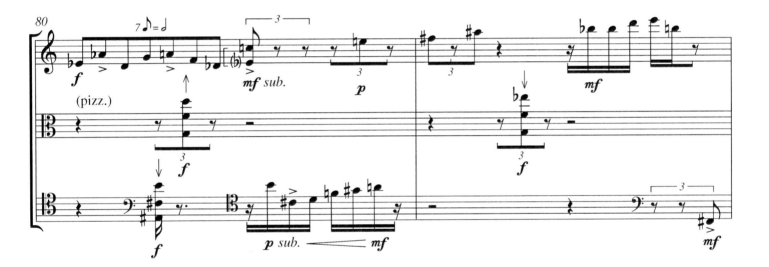

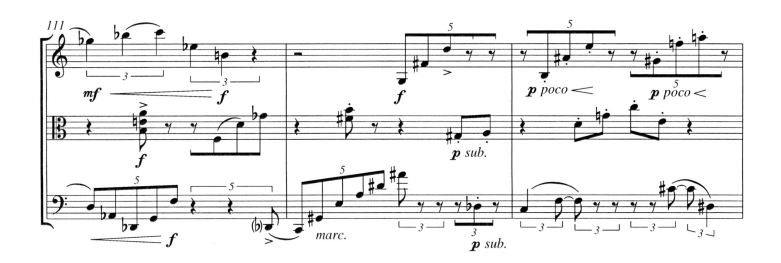

con intensità

NYC May 30, 2011